Encountering God

A Devotional for the Kingdom Driven Entrepreneur ™

Shae Bynes

Co-Founder, Kingdom Driven Entrepreneur

KingdomDrivenEntrepreneur.com

Encountering God: A Devotional for the Kingdom Driven Entrepreneur

ISBN 978-0989632225

Published by Kingdom Driven Publishing
4846 N. University Drive #406
Lauderhill, FL 33351

Printed in the United States of America

Cover art by Nibrima Branding & Design
www.nibrima.com

Acknowledgements

Lord, I thank You from the depths of my heart for Your faithfulness, Your constant direction, and Your grace as I stepped out in obedience and way out of my comfort zone to write this devotional. I had no earthly idea what I was doing, but I'm grateful that You are the most amazing teacher and always know what You're doing. Thank You in advance for every life that is changed as a result of this devotional. All of the glory belongs to You!

To each Kingdom Driven Entrepreneur family member who took time to share your story with me, thank you so much! While I was unable to use every story that I heard, I was so blessed by each of them and appreciate your transparency and generosity to share for the benefits of others. This thank you goes to Bess Blanco, David and Tanisha Burrus, Jeanette Burton, Jeff and Dawn Clark, Kelli Claypool, Crystal DeLoach, Candace Ford, LaTara Ham-Ying, Barbara Hemphill, Alicia Hommon, Amos Johnson, Donna Marie Johnson, Maria McDavis, Lisa Miller-Baldwin, Alex Navas, Heather O'Sullivan, Lenika Scott, and Steven Washington.

To my other half and my very best friend Phil Bynes, thank you for your ongoing encouragement, your prayers, your wisdom, and your love. I am so very blessed to be your wife.

To my sister Stacye Brim, thank you for your support, feedback, and wonderful editing skills. You're the best -- love you!

To my sister and Kingdom Driven Entrepreneur Co-Founder Antonina Geer, I couldn't ask for anyone better to be on this amazing journey with. I thank God for you in my life. Love you so much, sis.

Foreword

As you go through life there will be instances when you will know beyond a shadow of a doubt that you've experienced a God moment. One of those moments for me is the very first conversation I had with Shae Bynes. What started out as just an introductory phone call turned into a two hour call sharing about God's goodness, our desire to be used by God for the benefit of His people, and the purpose He's placed on our lives. That initial conversation was the start of what is now a wonderful covenant friendship. It is a humbling honor to know a woman of God such as Shae -- one who has simply said "yes" to being used by God and whom I affectionately call my sister.

Although our journey of friendship started just a short time ago in early 2012, it is indeed one that was ordained by God. I wholeheartedly believe that it was a God moment when our paths crossed. In this time of knowing Shae I've had the privilege to see firsthand God moving in her life, maturing her in the Word, and clearly showing His uncontainable love for her.

To know Shae is to know that she loves to tell stories. And as one of her sisterfriends I'm often on the receiving end of her awesome storytelling. The stories I love most are the ones in which she shares of her encounters and experiences with God. I'm often amazed at how God speaks and relates to her. It's so awesome to hear these experiences as well as witness them up close and personal. From the moment she yielded her heart to to God in pursuit of more of Him, she's been able to experience Him in ways that she has never experienced Him before.

Similar encounters with God can happen for you as a Kingdom Driven Entrepreneur. Your relationship with Him can be so much more than what you currently see or experience. Most of us have yet to tap into the magnificence of His love for us and the abundance of wondrous works He desires to rain in our lives. As entrepreneurs of faith we tend to keep God in a box, oftentimes thinking that the way He talked and walked with people in the Bible can't possibly be experienced in this day and age. Or that what we see Him do in the lives of others can't be experienced in our own lives. Oh, but that and so much more could be evident in our lives, businesses, and ministries when we seek after it. However, we have to be willing and open to knowing more than the God of yesterday and begin to desire to experience Him in the fullness.

I believe that this book will provide you with what you need to move past the familiar and tap into who God truly is and who He desires to be in all areas of your life. It will guide you to develop a more intimate relationship with Jesus Christ that goes beyond the point of salvation. Through prayer and study this book was designed to take you through a 21 day journey of experiencing the very nature of God, Jesus Christ, and the Holy Spirit. From the testimonies of one-on-one encounters with God's power and love, to the characterization of Jesus Christ, to the personification of the Holy Spirit, you are in for a journey that will change your life.

God encounters are not just stories that happened in the Bible or something that happens to other people who may be perceived as "deep" or "very spiritual". Encountering God is available to all believers and entrepreneurs of faith. This devotional will show just how it's happening in the lives of everyday people and in extraordinary ways.

As you read this devotional yield your heart to God and all that He wants to show you. There is so much more to this Christian walk than just knowing about God. God desires for us to regularly experience the depth of who He is and His manifested presence here on earth, but you have to want it and be in constant pursuit of Him. God is awaiting you. He wants to show you His heart.

Antonina D. Geer
Co-Founder, Kingdom Driven Entrepreneur

A Word from the Author

The assignment to write this devotional was given to me during prayer shortly after we released our first book, *The Kingdom Driven Entrepreneur: Doing Business God's Way* in November of 2012. The Lord shared with me that the principles for Kingdom Driven entrepreneurship presented in our first book were absolutely key, but there was a need for a companion to that book because the number one thing we need as Kingdom Driven Entrepreneurs is an intimate relationship with Him and an understanding of the ministry of the Holy Spirit.

Too many of God's precious people stop the pursuit once they've accepted Jesus Christ as their personal savior. Yes, there is an amazing eternal benefit to joining the body of Christ, but God has so much for us to experience here on this side of heaven. Jesus even said it Himself...He came that we might have LIFE and have it more abundantly (John 10:10). He wants us to hit the bull's eye on His plans and purpose. He wants us to serve as ambassadors of His Kingdom. He wants to have encounters with us on a daily basis. Yes, encountering God is a lifestyle. It is not a one-time event nor is it an academic exercise.

That is why this devotional was written. As a Kingdom Driven Entrepreneur seeking to advance the Kingdom of God in the marketplace, you have an important assignment on your life. You can't fulfill all He wants you to do without experiencing Him in deeper ways and knowing His voice.

While this is a 21-day devotional, I encourage you to take as much time as you need with each section. Consider journaling when you read each section to record what the Lord is speaking to your heart. This will be very helpful for you to refer back to in the future. The first 7 days focus on the character of God. The second 7 days focus on the ministry of the Holy Spirit. The final 7 days are centered around how we make encountering God a lifestyle so that we are empowered to be living examples of His love and power to those around us.

My prayer is that this book will help you to cultivate a more intimate relationship with the Lord and experience Him in ways you never have before. Even as the author of this devotional, it has ministered to me deeply and I thank God for that.

God craves your attention and desires a relationship with you. James 4:8 says when you draw near to God, He will draw close to you. When you pursue the God of all creation and His presence, your life (and your business) will never be the same.

Day 1: God Is Faithful

"Understand, therefore, that the Lord your God is indeed God. He is the faithful God, who keeps his covenant for a thousand generations and lavishes his unfailing love on those who love him and obey his commandments." ~Deuteronomy 7:9 (NLT)

Maria McDavis has intimate knowledge of God's faithfulness. A life of drugs, sex, and abuse (physical, verbal, and sexual) led to Maria being locked up in prison from age 15 to 21. God had a plan. As part of the intake process at the prison, she had to take an IQ test as well as a number of other standardized tests. Her extremely high scores were suspicious, so she was asked to take the test several times to ensure that she wasn't cheating. Turns out that Maria was a certified genius. Instead of placing her in the GED program to get a high school diploma, the counselors in the prison placed her in an accelerated program and she finished 4 years of high school in 3 months time.

God had a plan.

After she finished high school, her counselor connected her with one of the most prestigious scholarship programs in the world that would provide her with mentorship and the ability to finish three degree programs, including an MBA in an acceleration fashion with some of the best universities in the world. The selection committee never should've considered her. She didn't have the grades, the money, the influential family or friends. In fact, she didn't even want to be a part of the program and attempted to sabotage herself during the selection process.

"I'm never ever gonna be nothing. I come from trash. I've lived in a trailer my whole life. I'm a drug dealer, a pimp."

God had a plan.

One person on that selection committee believed in her and showed her favor, and so she started the program. She continued to self-sabotage during her first year in the program. Her grades were poor and she should've lost the scholarship program and been kicked out of school on academic probation. A glitch in the software system at the university hid these facts and after a terrible first year, she was not kicked out of school and even continued to receive full scholarship funding for the program.

In the following years, Maria excelled academically, but she also lived a double life. After finishing multiple degree programs successfully, she went back into a life of pimping and drugs while working on her MBA. By day, she was a successful business woman generating tens of thousands of dollars a month, but by night she was snorting all of the money up her nose because of a cocaine addiction. As a single mom of

three children, she found herself without the money to feed them because it was all spent on drugs.
God had a plan.

She eventually married the father of her children and started attending church, but she was still struggling with these strongholds in her life. One day a woman from her church came by and brought her TD Jakes' Woman Thou Art Loosed Bible. She told Maria that she was led to come by and just let her know that she is loved. That was May 13, 2000 and the day that the Lord changed her life forever.

"It's funny how a lot of people get saved that way....when you're really down at the bottom. It's amazing how omnipresent and omnipotent He is. From the moment that woman left my apartment, I was able to connect every single dot on how God's hand got me to that point. I knew right then that I had to serve Him and there was no other option."

Within 7 days, she was completely clean and never looked back to drugs again.

God had a plan.

Maria wanted nothing more than to immerse herself in God. So much so that she abandoned her husband, disappeared on her business clients, and moved into her mother's home with her children. She spent the next year focused on taking care of her children, reading the Word of God, cultivating a relationship with the Lord, and actively going to church. After that year, the Lord told her that it was time to go back home to Los Angeles to reunite with her husband.

When she arrived back to Los Angeles, the Lord told her that she was forgiven but in order to be free from the bondage that the enemy would try to hold over her for the rest of her life due to her mistakes, she had to make retribution. She knew she had done a lot of horrible things to people and left several people hanging without any idea of where she disappeared to and why.

"I made a list right down to the people that I stole from for my drugs. I contacted every single one of them to make things right."

From those phone calls Maria made, she landed her first 6 clients for the new marketing consulting business she started.

God had a plan.

Even Maria's mentor who looked out for her during college immediately took her back under his wing, pulled in several personal favors, and helped her to network with others and learn how to interact socially with others.

"My vocabulary was bad. My clothing was inappropriate for someone who says they love Jesus. It took a period of five years to learn how to just operate like a normal person."

God is so faithful. The people who Maria committed the most relationship-damaging acts toward are the same people who helped her out the most and even continue to refer business to her this day. She went on to grow a highly successful marketing agency and is a dedicated wife and mother.

Maria admits that every day is a new challenge for her. She still struggles with trusting people and has to cast down doubt and insecurity on a regular basis. However, because she stands on the solid rock of Jesus Christ and spends time daily communing with God, she is able to faithfully move forward with the purpose and plan that God has for her as a faithful and loving wife, a dedicated mother, and an entrepreneur committed to transforming lives.

God will go to the lengths of the Earth and back to get a message to you if you simply have a willing heart. He cares so much for you that He pursues you, even when you don't realize it.

His faithfulness abounds in every area of your life, including your business. The more you recognize His faithfulness, the greater your faith will be. The greater your faith, the higher your expectations will be. The more you trust and expect God to be every single thing that He says He is, the greater the manifestation of His promises you'll experience in your life and business. While man is not always faithful, that bears no relevance to the faithfulness of God. God's faithfulness remains the same.

Say this prayer aloud:

"Father, I thank You for Your faithfulness. I know that You are all powerful, all knowing, and ever present in my life. Open my eyes so I may see both the small and big ways that You have displayed Your faithfulness in my life and business. Bring these moments to my remembrance by Your Holy Spirit so that I may stay encouraged and remain focused on how absolutely big You are. Thank You for helping me to recognize You and Your Hand in every aspect of my life."

Day 2: God Is Your Provider

"And my God shall supply all your needs according to
His riches in glory by Christ Jesus."
~Philippians 4:19 (NKJV)

Alex Navas started his first mortgage company along with his business partner at the young age of 21. Less than a year later he gave his life to the Lord, and it didn't take long for him to realize that something was going to have to change with his business.

"I had people at church coming to me and telling me that they couldn't do business with me because they heard who my partner was."

Unbeknownst to Alex, he was aligned with a partner who had a reputation for unscrupulous business activity. Alex was faced with a decision. He had grown a successful mortgage company making $20,000 to $40,000 monthly, but at what cost?

"I realized that I could no longer be aligned with my business partner. I wanted to do right by God and I couldn't expect him to continue to bless me in that business."

Alex was newly born again and decided that He was going to trust God to be God - Jehovah Jireh, his provider. He approached his business partner and told him he couldn't continue to work together in business.

He sold the entire mortgage business over to his partner for $1 (which he never received) and they went their separate ways.

Even though the mortgage company was financially successful, Alex and his wife had also increased their standard of living significantly and lacked financial wisdom at that time of their life, so they didn't have much savings. In fact, they had approximately $2,000 to their name and no additional income as his wife had been working alongside him in the mortgage business.

They wanted to start another mortgage company on their own, however in the state of Illinois it required that they have at least $50,000 in equity before opening the business. Alex decided to go work for a friend's mortgage company...and then the miraculous happened.

"God made a way. He showered us with $70,000 supernaturally over a matter of only 60 days. I still don't know where all of that came from, but I do know it was all God. That was God saying that He was going to meet me where I was at."

This miraculous provision made it possible for Alex and his wife to open up their second mortgage business and do business the right way.

"Whether it's the $70,000 or there have even been times when I just needed $2 for milk....He delivers. It's the same miraculous God whether it's $70,000 or a gallon

of milk or loaf of bread. He can't fall back on His character. He is a provider and He always comes through right on time."

I experienced God's supernatural provision in my own family's real estate investing business in the months following the launch of Kingdom Driven Entrepreneur with my partner Antonina Geer. The truth is that all hell broke loose in our real estate business and things that we had never experienced before were taking place. Repeated expensive repairs, multiple vacancies, a tenant who was a victim of check fraud which impacted his ability to pay -- everything happened at once and drained any extra funds we had completely dry over a series of months.

I believe to this day that all of this happened to serve as a distraction from doing the work He called me to do -- to equip entrepreneurs of faith to build thriving businesses so they can serve their families, truly impact lives, and advance the Kingdom of God. A distraction could cause us to speak negatively over the situation and pull me away from the work of Kingdom Driven Entrepreneur.

My husband and I kept pushing through, believe that God would work it all out, but we weren't sure how. We knew that we had a shortage of approximately $1,200 to cover real estate taxes for one of our properties. Typically the funds would have been set aside and available for taxes, but we had already spent our reserves dealing with the issues with the properties.

We wrote $1,200 along with the deadline date that we need the money on our whiteboard in the office, but had no idea where the extra money was going to come from in such a short window of time.

Around that time an opportunity came for us to do a quick real estate deal that would've yielded a minimum $5,000 profit. It seemed to be a certainty, but in the final hours it didn't work out. It was disappointing to be honest, but we knew God had a plan. What was that plan? No idea.

The day arrived for us to pay the bill and we were still $1,200 short. I sent my husband to the bank to get cashier's checks and see if he could negotiate with the tax assessor's office for the one property that we were short on. My phone rang. It was my husband:

"Honey, I'm looking online and it's saying that the bill has been paid and we don't owe anything."

We were confused. We discussed some possibilities of what could've happened, and I encouraged him to go to the tax office and see what was going on. A few hours later, my husband arrived home and placed a piece of paper in front of me. It was a receipt. Over $2,100 in real estate taxes. PAID IN FULL. The bill was completely paid by an entity other than ourselves. Instead of the increase coming the way we thought we needed it, God simply cancelled the debt entirely!

What an awesome God we serve! I kept a copy of the receipt. I circled the payment confirmation number in red and wrote a note of praise to God and placed it permanently in my journal.

He is Jehovah Jireh which literally means "the Lord who provides" and "the Lord who sees." He goes ahead and makes provision for you. He knows all of your needs and is able to meet them right in time, just as He did for Abraham by placing that ram in the bush to sacrifice instead of his dear son Isaac. Just as He did for Alex when he trusted Him by selling his mortgage business for $1 in order to move forward and do business God's way. Just as He did for my family as we walked in faithful obedience.

Meditate on Matthew 6:25-33 (NLT):

> "That is why I tell you not to worry about everyday life—whether you have enough food and drink, or enough clothes to wear. Isn't life more than food, and your body more than clothing? Look at the birds. They don't plant or harvest or store food in barns, for your heavenly Father feeds them. And aren't you far more valuable to him than they are? Can all your worries add a single moment to your life?
>
> "And why worry about your clothing? Look at the lilies of the field and how they grow. They don't work or make their clothing, yet Solomon in all his glory was not dressed as beautifully as they

are. And if God cares so wonderfully for wildflowers that are here today and thrown into the fire tomorrow, he will certainly care for you. Why do you have so little faith?

"So don't worry about these things, saying, 'What will we eat? What will we drink? What will we wear?' These things dominate the thoughts of unbelievers, but your heavenly Father already knows all your needs."

"Seek the Kingdom of God above all else, and live righteously, and he will give you everything you need."

All of this applies to your business. Believe that if God has called you to do something specific in your business, He has already made provision for it. Whether you see the manifestation of that provision at this exact moment is not the point. The point is that He has already provided, and it's important to trust Him at His word and keep stepping out in obedience. Do the absolute best with what you have where you are right now and continue to believe God for the increase. God will honor your faithfulness.

Say this prayer aloud:

"Lord, thank You for Your supernatural provision in my life and business. Thank You for surrounding me with Your divine favor and giving me favor with ALL men.

Open doors for me that no man can shut, and close doors for me that no man can open. Prosper everything that I put my hand to that is according to Your purpose and plan. I will not worry about everyday life or about this business You have called me to because I know that You are Jehovah Jireh - the Lord my provider."

Day 3: God Is Infinitely Wise

"Oh, how great are God's riches and wisdom and knowledge! How impossible it is for us to understand his decisions and his ways! For who can know the Lord's thoughts? Who knows enough to give him advice? And who has given him so much that he needs to pay it back? For everything comes from him and exists by his power and is intended for his glory. All glory to him forever! Amen." Romans 11:33-36 (NLT)

I often find myself looking up in the sky with a smile saying "God, you are so SMART!" To say that God is smarter than us is the understatement of a lifetime. He has an amazing way of orchestrating a series of events and circumstances that ultimately work together for our good and for His glory, even when we don't understand what is happening or why (Romans 8:28).

Lisa Miller-Baldwin, the founder of The Wonderfully Made Foundation in Oklahoma City, Oklahoma experienced God's infinite wisdom in a significant way in late 2012 and in 2013.

"We haven't received ANY large grants or millionaire donors, but we HAVE GOD!"

The Wonderfully Made Foundation started as an organization that provides empowerment for women who have suffered from domestic violence, but later expanded to fill a need for women and children impacted by homelessness. The foundation provides support systems, training, and housing to help them get back on their feet. Ironically, it was only months after Lisa launched the Wonderfully Made Homeless Home that she and her husband experienced homelessness up close and personal as a result of a house fire.

"I praised God because although most was lost, we were not killed or injured. But God left us a remnant in that; He saved our front loader washer and dryer!"

Lisa continued to stay busy with her foundation work, all while juggling the inconveniences of homelessness. She received support through personal donations as well as foundation donations, but the irony of her situation eluded her until she received a request for an interview from a local television station and sat in the chair to do the interview.

"I started to break out in tears when [the news reporter] was talking to me about the work of the foundation and my house fire. It was at that moment that I realized that I too was a victim of homelessness. Even though it was situational, I was considered homeless right now!"

That experience gave Lisa a greater level of insight and increased her empathy and sympathy for the families that she serves through the foundation. Because of her experience, she truly understood the reality of what homelessness looks and feels like. Not only did the fire help Lisa and her team to serve in a greater way, but it also opened new doors through both secular and

and Christian media to share the work of the foundation in the local community.

It was around this same time that the Lord gave Lisa an unusual idea to host a live event called Entrepreneur of Faith.

"I'm a logical thinker. I sat on the idea and didn't move forward for all the practical reasons. I wasn't willing to step out there because all of my personal financial resources (sometimes up to 90% of my resources) were focused on the Wonderfully Made Foundation."

But God in His infinite wisdom would not let it go and the idea kept popping up in Lisa's spirit. She decided she would step out in faithful obedience and plan the event even though she had no idea why the Lord wanted her to do it. Perhaps more notably she had no venue, no keynote speaker, no catering, no funding....nothing.

Lisa logged into her Facebook account and made an announcement that she would be hosting the event. God's provision kicked in immediately:

- A catering company sent her a message on Facebook offering their catering services (the largest expense of the event!) at no cost.

- When Lisa presented a proposal to the director of a beautiful venue she wanted to use for the event, the director was impressed and offered her use of beautiful venue she wanted to use for the event, the director was impressed and offered her use of their facilities at no cost. They even provided free tables for vendors and chairs.

- A printing company provided her with extraordinary pricing of only $300 for all of her marketing materials and 18-page conference booklets for all attendees.

- She secured David Green, the billionaire CEO of Hobby Lobby (and a man of strong faith) as a keynote speaker within mere hours of making a call to his assistant. He agreed to speak at the event at...you guessed it...no cost.

"This was my very first conference and my name is not Oprah Winfrey. But when God calls you to do something, He has His hands on it from day one."

God most certainly did. Nearly 400 aspiring and current entrepreneurs paid and registered to attend the Entrepreneur of Faith Conference in Oklahoma City. Lisa highlighted the work of the foundation during the event and received a number of donations. The event attendees were delighted at how the event was executed with such class and distinction.

It wasn't until a couple months after the conference ended that Lisa received the revelation that God wanted to use Entrepreneur of Faith as both a funding and awareness vehicle for The Wonderfully Made Foundation. The Lord has continued to open doors and is just getting started.

"He's so strategic. I think God doesn't want us to get grants right now. That way we can say we didn't have any of that, but yet He provided. This has increased my faith and reliance on God. It's not easy, and it is work, but along the steps of a righteous man, He will dictate the path."

The Bible tells us that it is absolutely impossible for us to understand His ways. The Apostle Paul gives us more insight into God's character in 1 Corinthians 1:27 when he tells us how God uses the foolish things of the world to shame those who believe themselves to be wise, and the powerless things to shame those who are powerful. The Lord Himself revealed through the prophet Isaiah that His ways are higher than our ways and His thoughts are higher than our thoughts.

Trust God. Rest in confidence knowing that whatever the Lord has called you to do in your business, He knows better than you do. Take a step in faithful obedience and watch your God (in His infinite wisdom) work on your behalf.

Say this prayer aloud:

"Lord, I recognize You to be all knowing. You already know the end from the beginning. Help me to remember that You are smarter than I am. Give me spiritual eyes to see things as You see them, spiritual ears to hear things as You hear them, and the faith to be obedient to Your calling when I can't see how the story ends. Help me, by the Holy Spirit, to walk in Your ways no matter how crazy it looks or sounds because I know that You have a perfect plan for me."

Day 4: God Is Your Loving Father

"All praise to God, the Father of our Lord Jesus Christ, who has blessed us with every spiritual blessing in the heavenly realms because we are united with Christ. Even before he made the world, God loved us and chose us in Christ to be holy and without fault in his eyes. God decided in advance to adopt us into his own family by bringing us to himself through Jesus Christ. This is what he wanted to do, and it gave him great pleasure."
~Ephesians 1:3-5 (NLT)

The pastor who was ministering at the women's conference on that September evening prayed for the nearly 1,000 women in the room. She asked us to have a seat and close our eyes while she asked God to help us to know Him in a more intimate way. She asked God to give us spiritual eyes to see and spiritual ears to hear. Then she was quiet.

A couple minutes later she asked us to stand up if we heard anything. I hadn't heard anything but silence. Then she asked us to stand if we saw anything. I hadn't really seen anything either. There were all these women in the room who were standing.

"Show ME something, Lord. I want to see You. I want to experience You like never before."

It was a bold prayer request made with a bit of angst, but I was hungry. Hungry for more of His presence in my life. I knew there was more. With God, there is *always* more.

Nothing happened.

The pastor moved on and was sharing some closing remarks. I honestly cannot remember what she was talking about. What I do remember is falling to the floor. I landed right on my friend's beautiful white high heeled shoe....a serious face plant. Nose to shoe.

I didn't understand why I was on the floor. I tried to get up, but I couldn't move. It was as if my entire body was glued to the floor with rubber cement. I felt awkward and horribly self-conscious. I wondered what the people who were around me were thinking.

"Why am I on this floor? Lord, let me up!"

Nothing. I still couldn't move. I struggled for what seemed to be an eternity and then decided to stop.

"Ok, you have my attention. What do you want to tell me?"

Once God had my attention, He showed me something amazing. He showed me a vision of me playing the trust fall game as a child. The purpose of the trust fall game is to trust that the person standing behind you will catch you when you fall. You close your eyes and fall backwards and hope for the best. The Lord showed me that when I played that game as a child I would fall backwards, but then at the last moment I would put my hand back to brace myself in case of a fall.

He told me that is what I did with Him. I trusted Him enough to fall backwards, but at the last minute I'd brace myself for a fall, thinking that I needed to take control.

He whispered to me: *"Do you know why you do that?"*

"No Lord, why?"

His response: *"Because you have no idea how much I love you."*

The rubber cement disappeared and I was able to get off of the floor. I thanked God for showing up and sharing with me in such a clear way and went back to my hotel room to go to bed.

The next morning, I woke up early. My roommate (the one whose shoe I landed on) was awake, so I shared more about what happened the evening before. I was in awe over the entire experience and we just sat there in our beds talking about the goodness of God. In the middle of our conversation, a heaviness fell in the room unlike I had ever experienced. There was a tangible presence of God in that room and all either of us could do was get on our faces and worship Him. As I worshipped Him and thanked Him for His presence, He showed me yet another vision.

He showed me a hand. The hand was opening and closing repeatedly. The Lord said to me, *"This is what man does. Sometimes his hand is open to you, sometimes it is closed. This is what you think that I do, but I am not man."*

He then showed me a vision of an open hand and said, *"THIS is me. I LOVE you and my hand is always open to you. Everything you need I have and am willing to give to you."*

What a loving Father. He is Abba Father. Over the next two weeks He showered me with more evidence of His love for me through signs, wonders, and miracles that I had never experienced before in my life. I wrote them all down in a journal because I never wanted to forget what God did for me. There is no way that I can ever deny His power, His love, and His presence in my life. It is undeniable.

You can't see Him, yet He's not distant. He's always present. You can't touch Him, yet you can feel a touch from Him. He loves you and no matter what you may think, He is not angry with you. Nothing -- absolutely nothing can separate you from the love of God (Romans 8:38).

God IS love (1 John 4:8) and there is no way that we can truly comprehend the breadth, the depth, or the lengths of that love that He has for us as His children. Whether you have a terrible relationship, a wonderful relationship, or no relationship at all with your earthly father, that relationship will never serve as an adequate or representative model of the love that God has for you. God's love NEVER fails (Psalm 136, 1 Corinthians 3:8).

Say this prayer aloud:

"Father, I thank You for Your love. You knew me and loved me even before You made the world. Your Word says that You have even taken the time to count every one of the hairs on my head! Thank You for loving me so much that you care about every detail of my life. Thank You for showing me my worth to You and my worth IN You. Help me to better understand – both in my heart and in my spirit – the reality of how great Your love is for me."

Day 5: God Is Your Protector

"The Lord is my rock, my fortress, and my savior; my God is my rock, in whom I find protection. He is my shield, the power that saves me, and my place of safety. He is my refuge, my savior, the one who saves me from violence. I called on the Lord, who is worthy of praise and he saved me from my enemies."
~ 2 Samuel 22:2-4 (NLT)

It was hot summer day and Steve Washington was enjoying life as a new father of a 3 month old daughter and owner of a thriving and highly profitable real estate investing business. As he did on a typical weekday, he went into his office in north Philadelphia, along with his business partner and five employees.

It wasn't often that they would have clients come into their office, but on this particular day two men came in and wanted to discuss their interest in purchasing a property.

"Everything in me said that these guys weren't real investors. Nothing added up. They didn't ask the right questions."

Despite his suspicions, Steve and his partner answered all of their questions and then walked them out of the office. Steve's partner left the office and then there was another knock at the door. This time it was Steve's wife and baby daughter with lunch in their hands. He welcomed the surprise and took his family into his office to enjoy a nice quiet lunch.

"All of a sudden I hear all of these people running up the steps and screaming. I hear violent voices saying 'Where they at? Where they at? Where's your boss? Everybody down! Everybody...get on the ground!'"

Steve was paralyzed by fear. He didn't know what to do. There was no money in the office to give them. He didn't know whether to leave his family behind to go see what was going on or to stay in place. He didn't want his daughter to start screaming or crying and call attention to their location. He started to think about his all women staff. He couldn't just leave them on their own.

"I tried dialing 911, but my phone made this really loud beeping sound when I dialed! Whose idea was it make phones make a noise like that during an emergency? I hung up the phone."

Steve then heard people running down the stairs and heard one of his employees scream out that one of the interns was downstairs and could be in danger. At that point, Steve knew that he couldn't stand still any longer. He hid his wife and daughter in the closet and left the room. His entire staff was lying on the floor. They shared with him that five men came in with five guns...and two of those men were the same ones who came into the office earlier that morning pretending to be interested in purchasing investment property. They were no longer on the premises.

He was safe. His family was safe. His staff was safe. However, the hand of God and His divine protection in the entire situation did not go unnoticed.

"I was in a room with NO door. It was also the same exact room that the guys had sat down in earlier that day for 25 minutes. I actually saw their shadows. I was waiting for them to come in. It wasn't a matter of IF, it was a matter of WHEN. There wasn't even a door! The office area was only maybe 1300 square feet. From a purely logical standpoint, it makes no sense that they didn't find me and my family."

The gunmen never bothered to come into Steve's office area. They went into the storage space, into his business partner's office, and they even broke down a bathroom door in an attempt to reach one of the staff member's who locked herself in there.

Yet they didn't think to go back to the same room where they spent 25 minutes earlier that day. Steve asked his staff why they didn't tell the gunmen where he was in order to save themselves, but they said they knew he just had a baby and didn't want to jeopardize his family.

"A cliché is a cliché until it happens to you. Then it's not a cliché anymore. I'd hear church people often say phrases like 'God will make a way out of no way.' It just seemed so cliché to me. But then when God DOES make a way out of no way, you're ready to go out and wear your 'Thank You, Jesus' hat!"

In the Old Testament days, it was common when someone had a powerful experience with God to build a pillar in honor and remembrance of the event. This incident served as a pillar for Steve. No matter what else happened in his life, he could never take away the fact that God protected him and his family.

It was just a few years later when Steve was able to add a second pillar. In 2012, on a flight back from Florida after a wonderful birthday cruise for his wife, they were faced with another brush with death. The flight was initially delayed for several hours and Steve and his wife Joy almost missed the flight because they weren't at the gate when the plane was finally ready for departure. They were the last passengers on the flight. They quickly walked past all the annoyed faces and found their seat.

During the flight they fell asleep, but woke up as they felt the plane begin to free fall.

"Usually during turbulence, the plane will free fall and by the time you count 1...2...3... you're good. During this free fall you could count to 15. I could feel the plane picking up speed as the nose of the plane angled down."

The pilot apologized repeatedly and announced that everyone needed to put on their seatbelts. The issue seemed to get under control, but then another free fall happened...twice. The pilot announced that one of the instruments on the plane was malfunctioning earlier, but now it was completely down and they were going to prepare for an emergency landing in Baltimore.

The pilot told all the passengers that the landing in Baltimore would take place in 15 minutes. The plane was coasting downwards and Steve could look out the window and see the city. Fifteen minutes passed.

Another fifteen minutes passed. The pilot was pulling the plane down, but it kept rising back up. She continued to attempt a descent, but the plane would not cooperate and Steve began to worry that the plane would run out of gas.

"My wife was crying. I was beginning to think I may not see my three daughters again. I quoted every promise scripture that I could think of to my wife. I quoted scriptures that didn't even apply. I was quoting so many that I couldn't think of any more. I wanted my faith to kick in. I kept singing:

'Jehovah Jireh, My provider
His grace is sufficient for me, for me.
My God shall supply all my needs.
According to His riches in glory....
He will give His angels charge over me'

I sang it over and over again the entire time."

When their plane landed in Baltimore, Steve was so grateful to be alive. Rather than taking another flight to Philadelphia, he and his wife rented a car and drove home. Steve reflected on the fact that he and his wife were the last people on the flight. They almost missed the flight. Could it have been that their words of faith or their presence on the plane played a part in the eventual safe landing of the flight?

God is your protector. In Psalm 138, David praises God for preserving his life in the midst of trouble, delivering him by His right hand, and stretching out His hand against the wrath of His enemies. That is the God you serve.

Stand in faith in times of turmoil – not only in life threatening situations, but also in difficult circumstances you may face in your business. Stand on His promises in confidence, knowing that He is your refuge. He is your strength and a very present help in trouble (Psalm 46:1).

Equally important is recognizing God's hedge of protection that keeps devastating occurrences from happening to you in the first place. You have absolutely no idea how often His angels have kept guard over you and intervened on your (or your loved one's) behalf. He deserves praise for that and so much more!

Say this prayer aloud:

"Thank You Lord for being my refuge and my place of safety. Thank You for Your faithful promises that serve as both my armor and protection. I stand on Your Word that says that though a thousand may fall at my side and ten thousand may be dying at my right hand, that no evil will touch me. Thank You for ordering Your angels to protect me wherever I go. You are my rock and in You only will I trust."

Day 6: God Is Your Restorer

"Instead of shame and dishonor, you will enjoy a double share of honor. You will possess a double portion of prosperity in your land, and everlasting joy will be yours." ~Isaiah 61:7 (NLT)

Health coach Bess Blanco and her siblings grew up in a fundamentalist Christian cult; one leader and a lot of rules, manipulation, mental abuse, and sexual abuse.

"The air was heavy all the time. I distinctly remember feeling spiritual darkness around me. It was so tense. There was a lot of fighting in my home with my parents and there was so much crying. Turmoil is a good word to describe it. No peace. Not much joy because it was sucked out of the air."

Despite the difficulties and the religious shackles placed on Bess, she always had a personal intimate relationship with Christ. She accepted Jesus as her personal savior at the young age of 5. Quite the dreamer, she often laid down on the grass outside looking at the sky and just marveled at Him and spoke to Him. He was her best friend, but because of the religious abuse she experienced, she often suffered from guilt and would beg the Lord to forgive her.

When Bess was 10 years old, she experienced a significant moment with God that gave her light in the midst of her darkness. She woke up abruptly from a disturbing dream and the Lord showed her an angel praying at the foot of her bed. She instantly felt a sense of peace wash over her and was able to go back to sleep. It was a moment she says she will never forget.

When she turned 11 she started to plan her escape and on her 18th birthday Bess packed her things in her car, drove away, and never looked back. Leaving the rigid and abusive religious environment opened up an entire new life for Bess and she began on a journey to absolute and complete freedom in Jesus Christ.

"I began to hear an entirely different theology. I also started to see other believers experiencing victory in their lives and speaking life. It was a VERY long process of healing, but it began when I left that place and started to develop a whole new side of my relationship with Him."

God will meet you right where you are and restore your soul (Psalm 123) and the joy of your salvation (Psalm 51:12).

Bess moved in with her brother and started college. Six weeks later she met Juan. They were fast friends and quickly decided to get married. They started a family, but several years into the marriage while in her late 20's, Bess was struggling with bitterness in her heart and made a series of bad decisions. She walked away from both her husband Juan and the Lord after 10 years of marriage. They separated for a few months and then officially divorced in December of 2006. It was one of the most painful times of Bess' life, but God didn't allow her to stay far from Him for long and a month later she renewed her relationship with Him.

"He kept drawing me back. It was like He was jealous for me! I was His kid, His bride, and it was like He couldn't live without me! It was really amazing!"

Over the next several months, Bess and Juan went through a difficult time. They fought in court over custody of their children all while Bess was dealing with a seizure disorder that caused seizures that lasted for several hours and could only be stopped via medically induced comas.

But God. In the summer months after the divorce, the Lord used Bess' illness to soften Juan's heart towards her. That began a journey of healing in their relationship that was nothing short of supernatural.

"We knew we were supposed to be together. God softened our hearts towards each other. I was suffering from this seizure disorder. I couldn't drive. I couldn't work."

Later on that year they were remarried and now, several years later, they stand strong building their family and serving together in ministry.

"The fact that I am healthy, alive, able to minister to others, and a good mom today...it's crazy. Only God can explain that."

Your God has restoration power. Whatever your enemy the devourer has stolen, God desires to restore it whether it be your health, your personal or business finances, your property or land, your relationships, or your joy.

He spoke through the prophet Joel and said "*I will give you back what you lost to the swarming locusts.*" (Joel 2:25 NLT) He spoke through the prophet Isaiah and said "*Instead of shame and dishonor, you will enjoy a double share of honor. You will possess a double portion of prosperity in your land, and everlasting joy will be yours.*" (Isaiah 61:7 NLT)

Isn't that awesome? Not only does your God specialize in restoration, but He also specializes in multiplication and desires to make things better than they were before.

Proverbs 6:31 refers to a sevenfold restoration when a thief is caught. And remember Job? God blessed him with a double portion.

You may be thinking "Well, it wasn't the enemy who was the problem....it was me." Perhaps it was your careless actions that led to damaged personal or business relationships. Perhaps it was immaturity, disobedience, or a lack of due diligence that led to a significant financial loss in your business. God desires to restore regardless of whether it was the enemy (i.e. unfortunate circumstances or generational strongholds) or yourself. Why? Because He loves you without measure. Yield yourself to Him and stand in faith that His restoration power be manifested in your life.

Say this prayer aloud:

"Thank You Lord for being the Great Restorer in my life. I believe that You're the same yesterday, today, and forever so I speak Your restoration power in my life. I thank You that not only will You restore, but that You will bring increase and multiplication with it. Renew my mind Lord so that I may release any feelings of condemnation over mistakes that I've made. Your power works best in weakness and my heart will not be troubled because Your grace is all that I need."

Day 7: God Is Your Healer

"But if the Spirit of Him who raised Jesus from the dead dwells in you, He who raised Christ from the dead will also give life to your mortal bodies through His Spirit who dwells in you." ~Romans 8:11 (NKJV)

Remember health coach Bess Blanco? Her life's journey testifies in a very significant way that the Lord is still in the healing business. He is not only willing, but more than able to heal and restore physically, mentally, emotionally, and spiritually.

"I am a walking talking testimony of God's healing in so many areas."

Bess' story of restoration is incomplete without sharing the healing that took place in her physical body. Bess suffered from a debilitating seizure disorder. She had a series of seizures that lasted for up to 8 hours. The seizures almost killed her because her heart rate was so high. Medication wouldn't stop the seizures so doctors would place her under a medically induced coma. Five days later, she would come out of that coma and not remember what had happened just days earlier.

"It's a terrible and humiliating disorder. It was very traumatic. You lose all bodily functions. It was also lonely. Nobody really knows how to react to you."

Shortly after giving birth to her daughter, Bess suffered yet another seizure, but it was also her last. At the time of the seizure she was with her spiritual mother who told Bess that enough was enough and that this sickness had no right to destroy her life.

Bess went to mid-week service and went to the altar for prayer.

"There were people all around me praying for me. My pastor laid hands on me, but then the pastor's wife said 'Something is hindering your healing....and it's unforgiveness.'"

Bess ran home that evening, got on her knees, and asked the Lord for help.

"I said 'Holy Spirit I need your help because I can't forgive these people'. It was the people who turned on me at my hardest times, had abused me as a child, fought me in court for my own children, and there was all this pain. I started naming the names. I'd say each name and then say 'In Jesus' name I forgive you'. I was on cloud nine getting rid of that heavy burden whether I got healed from the seizure disorder or not."

The next week Bess went back to mid-week service and asked for prayer again. The pastor laid hands on her and let her know that he was going to lay hands on her until the healing manifested. The pastor's wife stepped in again:

"The pastor's wife said, 'There is only one more person that you haven't forgiven.' It was me. I needed to forgive myself. I started bawling and the moment my pastor

laid his hand on me and called that sickness out, I felt a puff of air leave my head and my shoulders. I physically felt something puff out of me and that's all I know. I don't know what it looked like or anything like that...but I was free."

This was an 18 month period of sickness for Bess, but it was also an 18 month journey of building her faith, exploring the word of God, and renewing her mind.

"I had to replace my old, nasty, and shameful thoughts of guilt with what the word of God had to say about me."

Seizure disorders are not easily diagnosed and there is no way to confirm medically that she is completely healed, however Bess stands in faith on this healing.

"I literally had to step outside [that church] and believe God that what had taken place was real and that what the word of God said about me was real, and that I was going to walk out my manifestation. I had to believe that."

Five years since this encounter with the healing power of God, Bess continues to be seizure free and takes no medication. While she suffers from the occasional moment of fear, she combats that fear by speaking the Word of God -- 2 Timothy 1:7 tells us that God has not given us a spirit of fear, but of power, and of love, and of a sound mind.

"A sound mind matters to someone who lost their mind. When I replace my fear with that scripture I feel the peace of God. It's like He's saying 'I got you, baby.' He is amazing!"

In Exodus 15:22-26, the Lord declared to Moses and the Israelites that He is Jehovah Rapha, the Lord who heals and promised them that if they did what was right and obeyed His commands that He would not make them suffer from any of the diseases that He sent upon the Egyptians. Not only is He Jehovah Rapha for the Israelites, but He is the same for you.

It is God's will that you be whole and healed from any infirmity that attacks your body...and He doesn't just heal some of your diseases, but ALL of your diseases. When Christ came, He healed everyone who came to Him because it was the will of the Father. Meditate on the following scriptures to confirm God's will.

> "Bless the Lord, O my soul;
> And forget not all His benefits:
> Who forgives all your iniquities,
> Who heals all your diseases"
> Psalm 103:2-3 (NKJV)

> "Yet it was our weaknesses he carried;
> it was our sorrows that weighed him down.
> And we thought his troubles were a punishment
> from God, a punishment for his own sins!"

"But he was pierced for our rebellion,
crushed for our sins.
He was beaten so we could be whole.
He was whipped so we could be healed."
Isaiah 53:4-5 (NLT)

Don't for one moment believe that you have to live with sickness in your body. You don't. Don't for one moment believe that God -- your Jehovah Rapha -- has placed sickness in your body in order to teach you a lesson. He's not a child abuser or the author of sickness.

God is a healer and a restorer. He will heal your heart, your mind, your emotions, your physical body, your relationships. Even if you're suffering from a disease caused by sin, disobedience, or negligence, confess to God. His grace abounds and nothing is impossible for Him.

As a Kingdom Driven Entrepreneur, your mission field is the marketplace and you will need to walk in good physical, mental, and emotional health to be most effective in serving others and fulfilling the specific purpose and plan that the Lord has placed in your heart.

Say this prayer aloud:

"Thank You Lord for being my Great Physician. Thank You for paying the ultimate price through Your son Jesus so that I may have life more abundantly and walk in divine health, both physically and emotionally. I recognize that You are bigger and greater than any pain or sickness in my body. Nobody is greater than You! When Jesus said "It is finished" it was indeed finished and I will rest confidently in Your finished work. I know without doubt that Your will is for me to be whole and in good health. I confess and repent of (any known sin, disobedience, or negligence) and I receive my healing now, by faith. Thank You Heavenly Father for loving me so completely and caring about every single thing that concerns me."

—

Day 8: The Holy Spirit Abides In You

"Do you not know that you are the temple of God and that the Spirit of God dwells in you? If anyone defiles the temple of God, God will destroy him. For the temple of God is holy, which temple you are."
~1 Corinthians 3:16-17 (NKJV)

The Spirit of God, the Holy Spirit dwells within you. The Lord said in Ezekiel 36:27, "I will put my Spirit within you so that you will follow my decrees." He placed His Spirit within you so that you can walk in His ways. The Holy Spirit isn't a force or a mysterious wind; He is a person. He performs actions like a person and relates like a person.

Because of the amazing love and grace from your Heavenly Father, the very essence of God remains in you and does not depart from you because you have accepted and received salvation through Jesus Christ.

Years ago I visited a Christian theme park in Orlando with my family called The Holy Land Experience. One of the most interesting things at the park was a huge indoor replica of Jerusalem and it was the first time I had a close view of what the Jewish temples were like. I saw the three courts -- the outer court, the inner court, and the Holy of Holies.

In Old Testament times, it was the outer court where the people would make their sacrifices to God and the inner court where the priests offered sacrifices to God (on behalf of the people), but the Holy of Holies housed the presence of God. Only the high priest was able to enter the Holy of Holies to offer blood sacrifices for the Israelites, and he could only do it once per year!

As I examined this replica of the Jewish temple, I was able to understand what the apostle Paul meant when he said that our bodies are temples of God. I heard a minister explain how we are modern day temples; our bodies (our flesh) are like the outer court and our soul (mind, will, and emotions) are like the inner court, but our re-created spirit is the Holy of Holies which is where the Spirit of God dwells within us.

Why is this significant? Your enemy Satan has absolutely no access to the Holy of Holies, which is a huge advantage to you. When you yield yourself and allow the Holy Spirit to lead and guide your steps, everything you do that is born of the Spirit is off limits to the enemy.

Because the Holy Spirit abides you, you also have received the fruit of the Spirit (Galatians 5:22) which is love, joy, peace, patience, kindness, goodness, faithfulness, gentleness, and self-control. How do you cultivate that fruit? By praying persistently without doubt (Luke 18:1), seeking God with your whole heart (Jeremiah 29:13), praising and worshiping Him, meditating on the Word of God, and being in His presence. When you're in the presence of God, you can't help but become more like Him.

When you allow yourself to be led by the Holy Spirit it will be evident. It's that demonstrated character that makes it possible for you as a Kingdom Driven Entrepreneur to make Jesus Christ known in the marketplace -- it's not through quoting scriptures, putting scriptures on the walls of your office, or having a fish bumper sticker on your car. While those are good things, it is your character that will draw people to Christ - the fruit of the Spirit that abides in you on display.

Say this prayer aloud:

"Father, I thank You that not only are You with me, but You have placed Your Spirit within me to abide in me always. Help me to stay mindful of this amazing and precious gift You have given me -- to work in me, through me, and for me -- so that I would not be left on my own. Holy Spirit, have Your way in me!"

Day 9: The Holy Spirit Is Your Comforter

"I will not leave you comfortless: I will come to you."
~ John 14:18 (KJV)

In His last moments with the disciples, Jesus shared with them that the Father would give them another Comforter who would never leave them and would dwell within them. That Comforter is the Holy Spirit and He provides a peace and presence in our lives during the challenging times we face in our lives.

Kelli Claypool sat in her car in the courthouse parking lot for nearly 4 hours contemplating the cleanest and simplest way to end her life. Life had hit rock bottom. She was going through a terrible divorce. She was turned away from her leadership responsibilities at church. The people she thought were her friends had turned their backs on her, and on this day she had just received the judge's orders that she and her ex-husband would share joint custody, but their daughters would live with her ex-husband.

"I was embarrassed because moms never lost custody of their children unless they were unfit, which was NOT the case in my divorce. My ex-husband had the money. He had the power. He had the influence. We had a judge up for re-election and his platform was father's rights. I felt like life was no longer worth living, especially without my daughters.

I remember what Job went through and cried out to God, 'Why am I the modern day Job? I've lost my family. I lost my home. I lost my income. I lost my self worth. Why? What did I do so wrong that you would turn your back on me?'"

It was in that moment of desperation for an answer from the Lord that the Holy Spirit, the Comforter, delivered. A sparrow landed on the light pole next to her car. Over an hour later, the bird was still on the pole and it seemed as though the sparrow was looking down on her. The song "His Eye is on the Sparrow" came to her spirit.

> Why should I feel discouraged
> Why should the shadows come
> Why should my heart feel lonely
> And long for heaven and home
>
> When Jesus is my portion
> A constant friend is he
> His eye is on the sparrow
> And I know he watches over me
> His eye is on the sparrow
> And I know he watches me

"That's when I felt the Holy Spirit's comfort. That's when He was talking to my heart. That day was the beginning of a renewed mind, even though I didn't realize it. I was wrapped in the warmth of the Holy Spirit. I felt hopeless, but the Holy Spirit gave me hope."

The Comforter is there to strengthen your spirit and the Word of God is your anchor. In those challenging four years during the divorce, Kelli found comfort in the Word.

"The Holy Spirit comforted me countless times during my divorce. I stayed in Proverbs and Psalms a lot. I found comfort in Psalms 69:13-14 wherein it says, 'But I keep right on praying to you, Lord. For now is the time, you are bending down to hear. You are ready with a plentiful supply of love and kindness. Now you answer my prayer and rescue me as you promised. Pull me out of this mire. Don't let me sink in. Rescue me from those who hate me, and from those deep waters I am in.'"

Today, Kelli is happily remarried to her husband Julius, enjoys a wonderful relationship with her grown daughters and son, and loves her work as "The Unconventional Business Coach." She is grateful that even though things aren't perfect, through the comfort of the Holy Spirit she can press through regardless of her circumstances, disappointments, and challenges.

It's important to know that the Lord never said that life was going to be easy, but He did not leave you to fend for yourself because He loves you without measure. The Father has given you a Comforter, and no matter what it is that you're facing in your life or business, know that you are never alone.

Philippians 4:67 (NLT) says: "Don't worry about anything; instead, pray about everything. Tell God what you need, and thank him for all he has done. Then you will experience God's peace, which exceeds anything we can understand. His peace will guard your hearts and minds as you live in Christ Jesus." Cast your cares upon Him, and allow the Holy Spirit's presence to shift the atmosphere in the midst of your storm.

Say this prayer aloud:

"Father, thank You for Your unfailing love and faithfulness. Thank You for protecting me beneath the shadow of Your wings and sending the Holy Spirit to comfort me during difficult times in my life. Like David, my heart is confident in You. Holy Spirit, I invite You into every situation I face. Shift my focus and help me to remember that Your grace is ALWAYS sufficient."

Day 10: The Holy Spirit Speaks To You

*"Meanwhile, as Peter was puzzling over the vision, the
Holy Spirit said to him, "Three men have come looking
for you. Get up, go downstairs, and go with them
without hesitation. Don't worry, for I have sent them."*
~ Acts 10:19-20 (NLT)

I will never forget the day that I heard the Holy
Spirit communicate with me by audible voice for the first
time in my life.

At that time in 2009 and 2010, I was really
struggling with the decision of when to leave my
comfortable $96,000 paycheck and corporate career to
become a full-time entrepreneur. I knew it was God's will
for me to leave the corporate world, but my businesses
were not yet at the point of replacing my salary. In fact,
my business profits weren't even close to replacing my
salary, which is what I desired to accomplish prior to
stepping out for full-time business....but God had other
plans (as He often does).

I was in Orlando at an event called Extreme
Business Makeover. It was the last day of what had been
an awesome 3-day conference for me. I had the
opportunity to meet and speak with the late Zig Ziglar
and his beautiful wife. I met a number of people face to
face who I had only known via Twitter and Facebook
prior to the event. I learned quite a bit of great
information about building my business. It was definitely
time and money well spent.

As I was ironing my clothes preparing for the final activities at the conference, the Holy Spirit spoke one simple word to me -- "Go!" It was strong in my spirit and clearly a word from the Lord. I'd never experienced anything like that before. I looked up and said out loud "So you're telling me to do this. You've got my back, right?" Then the Holy Spirit (as the Comforter and Spirit of Peace) confirmed that all was going to be ok. In fact, more than ok. All the angst I had felt in the months prior about leaving my job before having my "safety net" of accomplishments in business completed all went away. It was time for me to step out in faithful obedience and move forward on His plans and purpose for my life.

I called my boss the next day and gave my 30-day notice. I left my career and nearly six-figure paycheck behind in May 2010 and haven't looked back a day since.

The Holy Spirit also speaks to you prophetically through others. There are many examples throughout the Bible of the Spirit of God speaking prophetically through man, and He is still speaking in this way.

"So Shae, when are you going to stop doing all of that other stuff?"

It was a simple but annoying question from a friend during a group mastermind business call. I brushed him off with a quick retort -- "Don't even talk to me about that!" I was involved in, and I was still holding on to a business that the Lord was calling me away from. I wasn't ready to let go. It became apparent within 48 hours that it was not just a casual annoying question from a colleague, but it was the Holy Spirit who was speaking through him.

I was on my bed enjoying a book when the Holy Spirit interrupted and spoke to my spirit. It went something like this: "So, when ARE you going to stop doing all of that other stuff?"

Over the next couple of days the Lord spoke to me during my quiet time with Him and gave me specific instructions on how I needed to transition to a full time focus on Kingdom Driven Entrepreneur. The Holy Spirit knows exactly how to get a message to you and is faithful to do it. You have to remain open to receive from Him.

There are times when the Holy Spirit may speak to you through visions. Jeanette Burton was seeking God for His direction with her business. She had her hands in a lot of different projects, but really wanted to make sure she was focused on His plan. During a conversation she had with a pastor about her situation, the Holy Spirit spoke to her through a vision of a tree.

"It was a picture of a tree which was me and my ministries. This tree had branches going everywhere. It was a very straggly tree in need of a good prune. The branches were the many good ideas and projects I've started, but didn't get to finish because of another idea that came. I think I am an idea junkie!"

The Lord shared with Jeanette that it was time to prune and begin to say no to things, but He didn't stop there. The Holy Spirit continued to teach Jeanette by bringing to her remembrance the stories of David and Paul and how they had good ideas (David wanted to build a temple for the Lord and Paul desired to travel to Asia to spread the gospel) but God had different plans for them.

"We do not see the BIG picture, but God does. God has a bigger purpose than we do. He uses each of us as a part of HIS big plan... not ours.

So I realized that I needed to step back and seek the Lord on what His ideas are and what HE wants ME to do. Also what of those things do I need to leave to others?"

Through that vision of a tree, the Holy Spirit helped Jeanette to identify her tendency to over commit and take on too much when sometimes there was work that needed to be left to someone else. She was then able to allow God to help her prune that tree so she could be more fruitful in her business and ministry.

Although the Holy Spirit can speak to us in an audible voice, prophetically through others, and through visions, one of the most common ways that the Holy Spirit communicates with you is via inner witness, or an impression or knowing in your spirit.

Inner witness is typically not a voice. It may be a thought that comes to you and other times it may manifest as more of a disruption of God's peace in your spirit (an agitation) that is alerting you to a problem or obstacle. What is amazing is that the Holy Spirit will guide you in every area of your life and business -- no matter is too big or small. He'll even reveal things to you such as where you left that important paperwork that you seemed to have misplaced!

Your Father is so faithful to give you the Holy Spirit to live inside of you and speak to you in a way that is perfectly customized for you. As you spend more time in the presence of God, acknowledging Him, offering your praise and worship, the more you cultivate discernment of whether the thoughts that come to you are from the Holy Spirit or from a source other than God.

Say this prayer aloud:

"Father, thank You for speaking to me about all matters big and small through the Holy Spirit. Thank You for giving me spiritual eyes to see and spiritual ears to hear from You. I thank You for helping me to recognize Your voice. I will wholeheartedly follow Your lead."

Day 11: The Holy Spirit Is Your Teacher

"But you have received the Holy Spirit, and he lives within you, so you don't need anyone to teach you what is true. For the Spirit teaches you everything you need to know, and what he teaches is true—it is not a lie. So just as he has taught you, remain in fellowship with Christ."
~ 1 John 2:27 (NLT)

Candace Ford distinctly remembers when the Holy Spirit helped her to understand the scriptures during a challenging time of her life. She had a child out of wedlock and the enemy had her convinced that God didn't love her anymore. Someone directed her to Romans 8, and although Candace read it, she didn't understand what it meant. She prayed and asked for understanding and the Holy Spirit delivered.

Candace loves watching courtroom dramas. One day through a vision, God showed her a court trial where she was sitting at the table and about to be convicted of her sin. Right before the jury was about to declare her as guilty, Jesus walked into the courtroom and said "I didn't do it, but I will go to jail in her stead. I don't want her to experience this. I will go for her." The judge agreed.

"Immediately I felt bad because I knew I was wrong and no one should have to receive my punishment, but Jesus looked at me and said 'Because I love you I will go, so don't feel bad (condemned), don't feel sad, but be free to

operate through me because nothing you do will separate you from my love....NOTHING!'

The Holy Spirit taught me almost like a Law and Order episode!"

After 20 years of working in factories, the Lord called Jeff Clark to leave his job, come home, and become an entrepreneur. Jeff and his wife Dawn had absolutely no interest in self-employment after witnessing both of their own fathers' substantial financial losses during their years as business owners.

Dawn remembers the discussions that she had daily with the Lord in her prayer closet at the time that He was calling her husband to quit his job. She shared the following story:

> "Every morning that I entered my prayer closet, I said, "Good Morning Father!" As soon as I sat down, He'd say, "Dawn, will you trust Me?"
>
> "Absolutely Father!"
>
> "Will you be poor for Me?"
>
> "OF COURSE, Lord! I will surely be poor for you."
>
> This went on for a whole week. On Friday, I said, "Lord, just HOW poor are we talking here?"
>
> The next morning as soon as I sat down He said, "Dawn, will you be rich for Me?"

Immediately I responded, "Oh FATHER, that's easy - if I could be a Christian and still be rich, of course I would. But I recognize a trick question when I hear one."

For the next 3 weeks, He asked me the same question every day. I remember saying, "Lord, if You are trying to change my thinking - then lead us to Truth - because that prosperity Gospel makes me want to throw up."

The Holy Spirit revealed to me, "I will teach you - for I DO have great wealth for you."

I argued and argued about that entrepreneurs NEVER have wealth - everything is hard and burdensome."

That's when I heard - almost as if Father had entered the room with me, "Trust ME - don't worry about anyone else, but Me."

As you can see, the Holy Spirit will meet you right where you are and teach you in a very personal way that makes sense just for you -- He knows how you're wired!

The Holy Spirit will also teach you and give you insights in areas where you're weak in your business. In fact, He will teach you a completely new skill if that's what it takes for you to accomplish His will for your life and business.

Alicia Hommon is the owner of Cake Whimzy, a boutique custom cake company. The Lord called her into this business despite the fact that she doesn't really like cake (she does love other sweet treats!) and she doesn't have any natural talent for artistry and design.

Her company website says the perfect cake is one part creativity, two parts yummy, and 100% "How did you do that?" Alicia will tell you that the answer to "How did you do that?" is the Holy Spirit. It's through the Holy Spirit that Alicia receives her creativity for the designs, the intricate details, and even flavors for her custom cakes.

"I am really not an artist. Every gift I have [in this business] is a gift from the Holy Spirit. The designing of the cakes is the scariest part of my business to this day. I have no formal education, even with the sugar work but I do have a voracious appetite to read and learn new techniques. I cannot do the quality of work that God has called me to do unless I wait on Him. I have always been a dreamer and I tend to dream in technicolor when the Lord is speaking to my heart through dreams.

My husband gets stressed out sometimes because I'm sitting and waiting when he thinks I should've started working, but I'm just waiting. Frequently I dream the design of the cake and each step of the way of how to create that cake -- it has just become a part of my process. I get the answers when I sit, close my eyes, and wait on Him. This has been so key to the success I've had to date in my business."

Isn't it awesome that you have a teacher living on

the inside of you? The Bible tells us that the Holy Spirit will teach you everything (John 14:25-26), reveal the deep secrets of God (1 Corinthians 2:10), and guide you in ALL truth (John 16:13).

You have a teacher who freely gives you the wisdom and the knowledge of Almighty God. Not only that, but in John 14:26, Jesus also revealed that the Holy Spirit will bring you in remembrance of what you've already learned!

As you're on this entrepreneurial journey, know that the Holy Spirit is inside of you and will teach you. He will literally transmit the knowledge of God to you in any situation where it's needed. He will give you wisdom to handle difficult problems in your business. He will teach you how to apply the scriptures in so many areas -- customer service, hiring/firing, product development, negotiations. There is no area of your business that He is unable or unwilling to teach you. He'll even teach you a completely new skill if that's what is needed!

Say this prayer aloud:

"Thank You Heavenly Father for not leaving me on my own. Thank You for giving me a Helper and a Teacher who dwells on the inside of me and guides me in ALL truth. Holy Spirit, teach me the ways in which I should go. Thank You for divine insight and revelation every time I open the Word of God. Thank You for supernaturally bringing back to my memory the scriptures I need when I am faced with challenges. I have a confident expectation that through the Holy Spirit I receive the knowledge of God that I need in every area of my life and business, and for that I am so grateful."

Day 12: The Holy Spirits Warns Of What Is To Come

"However, when He, the Spirit of truth, has come, He will guide you into all truth; for He will not speak on His own authority, but whatever He hears He will speak; and He will tell you things to come."
~John 16:13 (NJKV)

In the book of Acts, the Apostle Paul was in a hurry to get to Jerusalem for the Festival of the Pentecost and prior to heading there he stopped to meet with the elders of Ephesus for the final time. As he addressed them, he shared the following (Acts 20:23-24):

"And now I am bound by the Spirit to go to Jerusalem. I don't know what awaits me, except that the Holy Spirit tells me in city after city that jail and suffering lie ahead. But my life is worth nothing to me unless I use it for finishing the work assigned me by the Lord Jesus—the work of telling others the Good News about the wonderful grace of God."

The Spirit of God forewarned many of the prophets in the Old Testament and continued to do so through the New Testament as He did with the Apostle Paul regarding his ministry. Even today, the Holy Spirit remains faithful to reveal and help you to prepare for things to come.

In 2004, Dawn Clark's mother was diagnosed with uterine cancer and in the months prior to her death, the Spirit of God warned Dawn during her quiet time that there would be circumstances that would not permit her to attend her own mother's funeral. You can imagine that had to be a hard thing to hear!

"At the end of Mom's life, we were going down south to help my dad every other weekend to give him a break and deliver some pre-cooked meals. We did this for almost five months. We were scheduled to go one weekend and my husband, Jeff, had been feeling awful. He was certain that the stress of all this racing about was wearing on him, so he was trying to sleep more and eat 'gentler' foods. On Thursday morning, he woke up and said, 'I've GOT to get to the hospital now!'"

Dawn stayed at home with the children while her husband went to the hospital where he was told that he needed an immediate appendectomy. Since her family was scheduled to help out her father that weekend, she called her dad to let him know that wouldn't be coming.

"While I was on the phone I could hear Mom's breathing. She had entered what I would call the early stages of the 'death rattle.' I asked my dad if I was hearing correctly and he agreed I was."

Dawn's husband had the appendectomy on a Thursday morning and he went through a number of complications that led doctors to keep him in the hospital. That next morning on Friday, Dawn's mother passed away. Her father informed her that the funeral would be Sunday morning, but her husband was in need of a full time caretaker for 72 hours.

"We could find no one who could sit with him. NO ONE. I called my dad and asked if we could move the funeral just a bit so we could be there. He had no emotional strength left. He needed to do this quickly. He had been by her side 24/7 for all this time – doing everything. How could I deny him what he needed? He told me he understood Jeff's needs and insisted that I take care of him.

So...I wasn't in attendance to my mom's funeral. Had my Father not warned me all that time in advance I would have been broken beyond imagination. Instead, I was able to grieve, in the midst of great peace. ONLY God."

Dawn had another forewarning experience a few months after her fourth child was born. She was alone with her children while her husband was on a business trip for a few days. The first morning during her prayer time, she received instructions to pack a diaper bag and take it to the basement. She packed the bag and went down to the basement and the Holy Spirit led her to where she should place the bag.

After she and the kids ate breakfast, He told her to have the kids pack their backpacks with crayons, paper, books, snacks, and blankets and place them by the back door. Then again during naptime He told her to take some flashlights, a tape player with tapes of some of her children's favorite Bible stories and songs, a set of fresh batteries, and her husband's work light. She even received the specific instruction to plug the work light in. Shortly afterwards, Holy Spirit prompted her to fill their water cooler and take some snacks and her baby's car seat down to the basement.

Later that afternoon, it became apparent why this forewarning was needed:

"About 4 pm I knew it was time to gather the kids and take the sheets off the line. We had just finished that when I felt an URGENCY to get the kids in the door. I was wearing the baby at the time. It was still very sunny out. There wasn't a gray cloud in the sky. To say that my son wasn't happy about having to come in early is an understatement.

"I sent my son Jeffrey to help my daughter Deniecia get in while my daughter Danica and I grabbed the toys that were in the yard. While we were in the garage, putting toys away, I heard a semi driving down our alley. That was so odd! I turned around to see what was going on – and it wasn't a semi – it was the wind coming down the alley. I yelled to Danica "RUN!" She wanted to wait for me because I had the baby, but I told her to go as fast as she possibly could. Running against that wind, it wasn't very fast. I could barely run against it and she kept being pushed back toward me. I grabbed her and we both raced for the house, as best we could."

Just as Dawn and her children made it inside the house, the sky turned dark and within seconds quarter-sized hail began falling and the tornado siren went off. Dawn was able to calmly instruct her children to grab their backpacks and they headed down to the basement for a two hour party -- dancing, coloring, playing songs -- all while a violent storm raged outside.

"I don't even know that the kids were fully aware of what was going on. After a while, you really didn't notice the tornado siren that was going off, and because the work light was fully charged, it just seemed more like a party when the lights went out for all that time.

Through the whole thing, I just kept giving thanks to my Beloved, because while my bridegroom was away, my Bridegroom knew I was alone and He took care of it all. What could have been terrifying for the kids was peaceful, calm and easy. No stress for any of us. He is so very, very good to me! There wasn't even rain in the forecast...it was just my amazing Savior taking care of me. Blessed, blessed, blessed I am!"

This is yet another wonderful gift of the Holy Spirit and it is so important to be sensitive to Him. He may reveal something very specifically as He did for Dawn regarding missing her mother's funeral, or He may simply give you specific instructions to follow to keep you from a harmful or even fatal plot of the enemy.

These same warnings from the Holy Spirit can take place when you're making decisions in your business. Perhaps you're faced with a decision to partner or do business with someone, or a decision to make a substantial investment for your business -- the Holy Spirit may agitate your spirit about the situation. He may also reveal something to come in your business that will help you prepare for the challenge. Listen, pray, and yield. He will not steer you wrong. The Word of God says that He will guide you into all truth because He is the Spirit of Truth (John 16:13).

Say this prayer aloud:

"Father, I thank You for the ministry of Your Holy Spirit to reveal and warn me of things to come in my personal family life as well as in my ministry and business. Your Word says that the Holy Spirit speaks expressly and I thank You for helping me to be sensitive to His leading and instruction. Holy Spirit, You are welcomed in every area and aspect of my life."

Day 13: The Holy Spirit Helps You Pray

"Likewise the Spirit also helps in our weaknesses. For we do not know what we should pray for as we ought, but the Spirit Himself makes intercession for uswith groanings which cannot be uttered. Now He who searches the hearts knows what the mind of the Spirit is, because He makes intercession for the saints according to the will of God." ~Romans 8:26-27 (NKJV)

On a winter evening not long ago, I woke up abruptly from my sleep sometime between 2 and 3 AM. One of my dearest friends (and Kingdom Driven Entrepreneur co-founder) Antonina Geer was on my mind and it was weighing heavy on my heart. I didn't know why and I didn't want to call her in the middle of the night. I had just spoken to her earlier that day and everything was fine. I woke my husband up and told him that we needed to pray, but I had no idea why or for what.

Has this ever happened to you? Has the Lord ever nudged you in the middle of night and you wake up with the urge to pray for someone? Have you ever just "had a feeling" that you needed to pray -- for yourself, for someone (whom you know or perhaps don't even know), or for a situation? Have you ever felt that you needed to stand in the gap for your church, your city, your nation? As believers, we're often called to do these things. When that happens, how do you know what to pray for? Simply put....you don't.

The power of prayer is undeniable, but the truth is that you're limited in your natural ability to pray perfect, timely, and effective prayers. You have limited knowledge. The enemy may have plans underway that you have no foresight into. God is the only one with infinite wisdom and He has given you the Holy Spirit to make intercession and help you pray as you should.

The Holy Spirit knows exactly what is needed. He is in sync with the Father's will. When you yield yourself to the Holy Spirit by speaking in other tongues as the Spirit gives you utterance, you will pray perfect prayers. There are mysteries that man does not understand, but God does (1 Corinthians 14:2).

Yes, you have a supernatural prayer language. The Holy Spirit takes the plans of the Father, pours those plans into your spirit, and gives you a supernatural language to speak. Not only does this help you to pray the perfect prayer (the will of God), but it also edifies you and builds your faith (Jude 1:20).

During Antonina's first visit to meet with me in South Florida, we attended my local church for mid-week service. During worship, the presence of God was strong in the sanctuary and she began to pray.

"The Holy Spirit is always interceding when we're speaking in other tongues, but that night it was so clear to me that He interceded. While I was praying in tongues, I felt a shift in my abdomen. It was as if something moved back into place or something was

*being removed. I knew at that very moment I was being
healed of something I didn't even know was a problem!
When you experience the presence of God like that, you
cannot leave out the same way that you came."*

Antonina had no idea that there was an issue in
her abdomen. She didn't even know to believe God for
healing in that area of her body. By yielding herself to the
Holy Spirit and praying in other tongues, she gave Him
access to manifest God's perfect will in her body, which
was for her to be completely whole and healed.

On that one winter evening when Antonina was
on my heart, my husband and I prayed in tongues until
we felt peace in our spirits. Whatever the work that
needed to be done at that very moment...whatever the
will of the Father was concerning her, we could rest
knowing that through the ministry of the Holy Spirit, we
were able to pray that out. To this day, none of us know
the reason why. We just trusted God.

You already received the Holy Spirit when you
were born again and accepted Christ as your personal
savior, but it is so vitally important to take the next step
and receive the fullness of the Holy Spirit by being
baptized in the Holy Ghost with the evidence of speaking
in other tongues. Without embracing this aspect of the
Holy Spirit, you're operating in substantially less power
than you should.

If you have never received the baptism of the
Holy Spirit and the gift of speaking in tongues, say this

prayer aloud from a sincere heart:

> "Father, You say in Your Word that You are faithful to give the Holy Spirit to those who ask You (Luke 11:9-13). In the name of Jesus Christ, I ask You to fill me to the overflow with Your Holy Spirit. I believe that I receive it because I believe that Your Word is true. Thank You Lord for giving me a supernatural prayer language."

Now yield yourself to the presence of the Holy Spirit, and begin to speak. You will speak words that don't make any sense to your mind and it may only be a few words at first, but over time as you yield yourself more words will flow from your spirit. This is an absolutely amazing gift that will change your business and impact not only your life, but the lives of others the Lord calls you to intercede for.

As a Kingdom Driven Entrepreneur who seeks to advance the Kingdom of God in the marketplace, you need the Holy Spirit to help you pray! You want to pray the perfect will of God for your business before your meetings, during your car commutes, in the morning before you begin your day, as you strategize, as you create products and services, as you write that book, as you prepare for that speaking engagement, and as you consider partnerships and new business opportunities.

You also want to pray the perfect will of God concerning your employees, your clients/customers, and the regions in which you operate business. There are too many factors you know nothing about. You can and should pray in your native speaking language, but remember that you are limited in your ability to intercede (pray) effectively on your own. Fully embrace this gift of the Holy Spirit and you will walk in a level of power and authority like you've never experienced before.

Say this prayer aloud:

"Father, I thank You for this amazing gift of the Holy Spirit. Thank You for giving me a Helper to intercede on my behalf regarding everything known and unknown concerning me as well as others. Holy Spirit, thank You for searching my heart and removing everything that is contrary to the will of God. Thank You for creating the perfect prayer for me. I yield myself wholeheartedly to You."

Day 14: The Holy Spirit Gives You Power

"Now to Him who is able to do exceedingly abundantly above all that we ask or think, according to the power that works in us, to Him be glory in the church by Christ Jesus to all generations, forever and ever. Amen."
~ Ephesians 3:20-21 (NKJV)

The creative power of the Holy Spirit is made evident in the very beginning of the Word of God. Genesis 1:1-3 says "In the beginning God created the heavens and the earth. The earth was without form, and void; and darkness *was* on the face of the deep. And the Spirit of God was hovering over the face of the waters. Then God said, "Let there be light"; and there was light.

The earth had no form! It was empty! The Spirit of God -- the Holy Spirit -- was hovering over the face of the waters and at the moment God spoke "Let there be light", the Holy Spirit took chaos and created light and order. Meditate on that for a moment. That same Holy Spirit with creative power and ability abides in you.

Consider the prophet Elijah. He was just an ordinary guy, but when the Holy Spirit came on him, he called down fire from heaven, killed hundreds of prophets of Baal, and outran King Ahab's chariot in the same day...and surely the King had some of the strongest and fastest horses in the land! (See 1 Kings 18.)

In the book of Acts, Jesus' last words to His chosen apostles before He was taken to Heaven were "And when the Holy Spirit comes on you, you will be able to be my witnesses in Jerusalem, all over Judea and Samaria, even to the ends of the world."

That same Holy Spirit with transforming and enabling power and ability abides in you. Otherwise ordinary people are extraordinary with the Holy Spirit's power. YOU are extraordinary through the power of the Holy Spirit.

The demonstration of the Holy Spirit's power does not only take place within the four walls of a church. This power can be demonstrated in your home, in your business, at your job, in the grocery store, at the mall. The Holy Spirit gives you power and authority no matter where you are. He abides and works within you.

When David Burrus and his wife Tanisha found out that they were expecting their first child, they decided that there was no reason for Tanisha to experience pain in childbirth.

"We wanted to take God at His Word that says that we have been redeemed from the curse of the law through Christ (Galatians 3:13) and that my wife will be saved in childbearing if we continue in faith, love, and holiness, with self-control (1 Timothy 2:15)."

They read a book called *Supernatural Childbirth* by author Jackie Mize, and during every day of Tanisha's pregnancy they spoke against pain, complications, and anything that would hinder the birthing process or be contrary to the will of God. They spoke the Word of God daily, fully believing and resting in the power and authority they had as His children.

"The Word says that whoever says to this mountain, 'Be removed and be cast into the sea,' and does not doubt in his heart, but believes that those things he says will be done, he will have whatever he says. We believed that and God came through for us."

He most certainly did come through. When Tanisha began to feel pressure towards the end of her pregnancy, she told David that it was time to go the hospital. There was no pain, only pressure. By the time they arrived at the hospital, they told the nurses that they believed it was time for her to deliver. When they got her into the hospital bed to check her dilation, they confirmed with surprise that she was about to deliver the baby right at that moment.

They prepared the room with worship music and thirty minutes later, their son was born. No medication, no epidural, and absolutely zero pain. That's the power of the Holy Spirit working within. Not only did Tanisha have one painless pregnancy and childbirth experience, but three years later she had another one with their second son.

In Ephesians 3:14-21, the apostle Paul shared this prayer for our spiritual growth:

"When I think of all this, I fall to my knees and pray to the Father, the Creator of everything in heaven and on earth. I pray that from his glorious, unlimited resources he will empower you with inner strength through his Spirit.

Then Christ will make his home in your hearts as you trust in him. Your roots will grow down into God's love and keep you strong. And may you have the power to understand, as all God's people should, how wide, how long, how high, and how deep his love is.

May you experience the love of Christ, though it is too great to understand fully. Then you will be made complete with all the fullness of life and power that comes from God.

Now all glory to God, who is able, through his mighty power at work within us, to accomplish infinitely more than we might ask or think. Glory to him in the church and in Christ Jesus through all generations forever and ever! Amen."

That is powerful. Your God is able to do exceedingly, abundantly above ALL you could ask or think according to *His mighty power that works within you!* Thank you, Holy Spirit!

Consider this: What would you do differently if you had a true revelation of the power of the Holy Spirit that is within you?

How would you approach the things God has called you to do within your business?

What mountains would you be removing and casting into the sea?

How much of the enemy's foolishness would you permit to take place in your life?

How BOLD would you be about seeing the promises of God manifested in your life and the lives of those around you?

Say this prayer aloud:

"Father, I thank You for the creative, transforming, and enabling power of the Holy Spirit that resides in me. Give me true revelation through Your Word about the power that is within me. Help me have the faith that opens the door for the Holy Spirit to do things beyond natural human comprehension. Holy Spirit, I ask that You do the miraculous through me. I purpose to be a walking testimony of Your awesome power of which makes You irresistible to the people around me."

Day 15: The Power of Your Praise

"Let everything that has breath praise the Lord. Praise the Lord!" ~Psalm 150:6 (NKJV)

There is tremendous power in your praise. Praise God because He is worthy of it! He is the Alpha and Omega, the King of kings and Lord of lords, Creator, Provider, the Lover of your soul, Redeemer, and so much more.

When you focus your mind on His amazing goodness, it creates greater fellowship with Him and helps you put everything in its proper perspective. It takes your focus off of self and beholds Him. It increases your faith in God's promises in your life and it releases the power of God.

Consider examples of how the power of God was released through praise in the Bible:

- Paul and Silas sang praises to God while in prison so loud that the other prisoners could hear them and "suddenly" there was a great earthquake that shook the very foundations of the prison. The doors flew open, their prison chains were broken, and they were released from captivity (Acts 16:16-40).

- The Lord instructed King Jehoshaphat to put the praise team right on the front line of battle rather than the soldiers...and they were completely surrounded by a vast army of enemies! God spoke through a prophet to assure the King that He would fight the battle on his behalf, and the choir sang praises to God in the beauty of holiness "Praise the Lord, for His mercy endures forever." The results of their praise? Their enemies started fighting amongst themselves! The enemy was defeated and Judah had the victory (2 Chronicles 20).

God is still the same today and, in fact, you have a better covenant with better promises. If praise released the power of God back then, praise releases the power of God now.

When it comes to your enemy, praise is one of your most powerful weapons. He doesn't stand a chance when you praise and exalt God in the midst of any circumstance! Praise God every step of the way in your entrepreneurial journey. It is foolish to the world, but it will increase your faith and lead to greater breakthroughs and acceleration in your business.

Commit to a lifestyle of praise. The book of Psalms is a wonderful book to read to focus on giving praise to God. By reading the Psalms aloud and personalizing them, you will gain fresh insight into His goodness and have powerful words to speak even during difficult times.

Begin to praise God now for the manifestation of

the vision He has given you for your business. Understand that the work has already been finished and every resource you need has already been accounted for -- human, financial, or otherwise. By praising God now, you are activating faith and supernaturally shaking your prison foundations and releasing your destiny.

Say this prayer aloud:

"Father, I will bless You at ALL times. Your praise shall continually be in my mouth. When circumstances are good, I will praise You. When circumstances that are troubling come my way, I will still praise You because You are good and You're worthy of my praise! No one can measure Your greatness! Thank You for being a constant source of joy and strength in my life. You are amazing Lord, and I thank You for working all things together for my good and for Your glory."

Day 16: The Power of Your Worship

"But the time is coming—indeed it's here now—when true worshipers will worship the Father in spirit and in truth. The Father is looking for those who will worship him that way. For God is Spirit, so those who worship him must worship in spirit and in truth."
~John 4:23-24 (NLT)

The Word of God tells us that those who worship God must worship in spirit and in truth. True worship comes from within your spirit. It requires humility, reverence, and a yielded heart. He sees your heart and desires sincere worship and fellowship with you because He loves you.

Worship literally means "prostrating, bowing to and laying aside your own self and your own life" which means that it is more than singing a slow song at church.

Worship is not meant to be solely a once per week church activity, but rather a lifestyle. Sustained change comes from private worship, and it is powerful to enter God's presence with praise and worship on a daily basis. In fact, it is the most important business meeting you will have each day. It's a selfless act of giving to offer up your worship. Because God is so abundantly loving, He gives right back to you and pours out His Spirit. James 4:8 says that when you draw close to Him, He draws close to you. He refreshes you and realigns you with purpose.

There's something else amazing that often happens during this important business meeting with the Lord of the breakthrough. When you enter worship with a pure heart, offer up your soul (mind, will, and emotions), and just honor God, He gives you solutions. It's in your worship where you receive answers specific to all areas of your life, including your business. He'll even download new ideas in your spirit.

Where the Spirit of the Lord is there is freedom (2 Corinthians 3:17), and when you worship corporately or privately you should feel free to do whatever the Lord is leading you to do. You may be lying prostrate on the floor, lifting your hands, bowing down, praying or singing in the Holy Spirit. Follow the leading of the Holy Spirit. Bold obedience applies to worship as well!

There's something else to consider. Have you ever thought about your work being an act of worship? Yes, the way you serve others through your business should be an act of worship and it should bring honor and glory to God.

You have so many ways to worship your Heavenly Father -- by walking in obedience, meditating on the Word of God, praying, singing psalms and spiritual songs, and making music to the Lord in your heart (Ephesians 5:18-19). Continue to worship Him always, yielding to Him completely. When your life is an act of worship, you are operating in His plan and purpose and it's a beautiful thing.

Say this prayer aloud:

"Father, I worship You in spirit and in truth. I magnify Your name and honor You with all that is within me. Enlarge my heart and make me a true worshipper. Help me to express myself freely in worship and to make my work and my very life an act of worship to You. Holy Spirit, thank You for falling fresh on me. Have Your work in me so that I can partner with breakthrough."

Day 17: The Power of Your Confession

"A man's belly shall be satisfied with the fruit of his mouth; and with the increase of his lips shall he be filled. Death and life are in the power of the tongue: and they that love it shall eat the fruit thereof."
~Proverbs 18:20-21 (KJV)

In Mark 11:23, Jesus Himself said: "For assuredly, I say to you, whoever says to this mountain, 'Be removed and be cast into the sea,' and does not doubt in his heart, but believes that those things he says will be done, he will have whatever he says."

Self-help and personal development leaders often stress the importance of positive affirmations, but as a Kingdom Driven Entrepreneur the words you speak over yourself and over situations in your life and business should be a confession or affirmation of the Word of God as an expression of faith. As a believer, it's important to understand the benefits available to you so that you are equipped to speak God's will in those areas of your life. There are so many things that the Lord has already done for you and already made His will known about, so it's key to embrace and faithfully stand firm in these promises.

What are some of these universal benefits available to you as a child of the Most High?

- You are healed by the stripes of Jesus Christ (Isaiah 53:5, Psalm 103:3)

- You have a spirit of power, love, and a sound mind (2 Timothy 1:7)
- You have the peace of God guarding your heart and mind (Philippians 4:7)
- All of your needs are met according to God's riches in glory by Christ Jesus (Philippians 4:19)
- You will always triumph in Christ Jesus (2 Corinthians 2:14)
- You are free from condemnation (Romans 8:1)
- All things will work together for your good if you love God and serve Him (Romans 8:28)
- You have the love of God poured into your heart by the Holy Spirit (Romans 5:5)
- You are strengthened by God (Isaiah 41:10, 2 Corinthians 12:9)
- You are redeemed from the curse of the law -- meaning you're redeemed from disease, poverty, and spiritual death/separation from God (Galatians 3:13, Deuteronomy 28)
- You have the God-given ability to produce wealth (Deuteronomy 8:18)

Psalm 103:2-5 also gives you insight into your benefits:

Bless the LORD, O my soul,
And forget not all His benefits:
Who forgives all your iniquities,
Who heals all your diseases,
Who redeems your life from destruction,
Who crowns you with lovingkindness and tender mercies,
Who satisfies your mouth with good *things,*

So that your youth is renewed like the eagle's.

You have a powerful benefits package, and you don't have to continue to ask for these (or any other promises made to all believers) -- you already possess them through salvation!

It's also powerful to confess what the Lord has to say about you. He says that you are more than a conqueror (Romans 8:37), that you are the righteousness of God by Christ Jesus (2 Corinthians 5:21), that you are delivered from the power of darkness (Colossians 1:13), that you are a joint heir with Christ (Romans 8:17), that you are a new creature in Christ (2 Corinthians 5:17), and you are chosen, holy, and blameless before God (Ephesians 1:4) -- that's just for starters!

Be consistent and strategic in your confession. If you're facing a specific situation, find out what the Word of God has to say about the situation so that you can reinforce that truth in your heart and activate your faith.

Equally important as confessing your benefits as a believer and confessing what God says about you in His Word is to confess the specific promises the Lord has made to you during your personal time with Him. He has a unique purpose and plan for your life and for your business. There are things He will speak to your spirit or through a vision or through prophecy. When He makes a special promise to you, confess it regularly until you see the manifestation.

You have to believe these promises in your heart. Make confessions of the Word of God a part of your daily devotion time and use them as necessary throughout the day to cast down negative thoughts or any attack of the enemy. If He said it, He will do it. Stand in agreement with His promises.

Say this prayer aloud:

"Father, thank You for making Your will and Your ways known to me through the Word of God and the ministry of the Holy Spirit. Holy Spirit, give me revelation concerning God's promises in every area and aspect of my life as I read and meditate on the Word of God."

Day 18: The Power of Your Prayers and Fasting

"So He said to them, 'This kind can come out by nothing but prayer and fasting.'" ~ Mark 9:29 (KJV)

The Bible is full of examples of people who fasted and prayed for a variety of reasons. Faced with danger, Ezra prayed for guidance and protection of the people as they departed Babylon to go to Jerusalem (Ezra 8:20-23). David fasted during a time of distress after hearing that Saul and Jonathan were dead (2 Samuel 1:12). Daniel received a vision from the Lord after fasting for three weeks (Daniel 10:1-2). Jesus Christ Himself fasted for 40 days and 40 nights prior to being tempted by Satan (Matthew 4:2).

Simply stated, fasting and praying position you for a breakthrough. It does not move God. It is not a way to force God's hand, but rather it is a way to allow Him to do a work within you that positions you for a breakthrough -- it may be a spiritual breakthrough or a natural one such as financial breakthrough, relationship breakthrough, health breakthrough, or even a breakthrough idea or strategy for your business. Your time dedicated to humble fasting and prayer will bring a release of God's power and presence in your situation -- a personal revival!

It's important to recognize that His power is already made available to you. God is not holding it back, but you have to be in proper position to receive it.

Denying your flesh through fasting, coupled with prayer and meditating on the Word of God will help your unbelief and turbo charge your faith! When you allow your spirit to dominate over your flesh, you've essentially rendered the enemy powerless because he has no access to the Spirit within you.

Be led by the Holy Spirit regarding your fasting because it is more of a heart issue than an exact formula. You may be led to do a Daniel fast, a water and juice only fast, or perhaps even an absolute fast (be sure to seek medical and spiritual counsel first). You may feel moved by the Holy Spirit to fast for one day a week, one week a month, or even 21, 30, or 40 days straight. It is a personal decision between you and your Heavenly Father.

The Bible does provide clear instruction on other aspects of fasting. Jesus instructed (Matthew 6:16-18, New Living Translation):

> "And when you fast, don't make it obvious, as the hypocrites do, for they try to look miserable and disheveled so people will admire them for their fasting. I tell you the truth, that is the only reward they will ever get. But when you fast, comb your hair and wash your face. Then no one will notice that you are fasting, except your Father, who knows what you do in private. And your Father, who sees everything, will reward you."

One of the key things you will want to do before fasting is to determine your purpose. What is it that you're seeking? Is it for a specific breakthrough? Is it to experience Him in a more intimate way? Is to hear His instruction clearly on something you're facing? Be clear about what you're believing God for!

There are times you may face in your life and in your business where the answer will only be found through the personal transformation provided by prayer and fasting. Spiritual fasting takes your eyes off of yourself and your circumstances and places your attention precisely where it needs to be.

Say this prayer aloud:

"Lord, thank You for speaking to my heart regarding the things I should think, say, and do to be more like You. Thank You for providing me with a tool that helps me to dominate the works of my flesh, grow in my relationship with You, and release Your power within me. Give me wisdom as to how a lifestyle of fasting and prayer will glorify you and lead me by Your Holy Spirit to know the times in my personal and business life when I should seek You in this powerful way."

Day 19: Meditating On God's Word

"Oh, the joys of those who do not follow the advice of the wicked, or stand around with sinners, or join in with mockers. But they delight in the law of the LORD, meditating on it day and night. They are like trees planted along the riverbank, bearing fruit each season. Their leaves never wither, and they prosper in all they do." ~Psalm 1:1-3 (NLT)

If you want to live a full and abundant life as God intends for you, meditating on God's written Word is essential. All scripture is inspired by God (God breathed), teaches us what is true, and provides correction (2 Timothy 3:16). It illuminates your path (Psalm 119:105). It is transformational and equips you to serve and to be a blessing to others. It equips you to make Jesus Christ known in the marketplace (do a study on the entire book of Proverbs)!

There's a distinct difference between simply reading the Word of God and meditating on it. Meditating on His Word requires active attention and reflection rather than passive academic reading. Before opening up your Bible, ask the Holy Spirit to guide you and reveal the application of the scripture to your own life.

The truth is that you already meditate on things all day long. Consider what you meditate on. Are you meditating on what you cannot do or what you do not have? Are you anxious about your health or your children or your spouse? Are you anxious about that client who hasn't paid you yet? Concerned about whether that lucrative contract is going to fall through? Rather than meditating on those things, meditate on what the Word of God says.

For example if you're meditating on things that cause you anxiety, flip the switch and replace that by meditating on Philippians 4:6-7 which says "Be anxious for nothing, but in everything by prayer and supplication, with thanksgiving, let your requests be made known to God; and the peace of God, which surpasses all understanding, will guard your hearts and minds through Christ Jesus."

Go back and re-read Philippians 4:6-7. Read it slowly and think about each word or phrase.

Be anxious for nothing: God does not want you to feel anxiety about *anything*.

But in everything by prayer and supplication: He wants you to pray or petition Him humbly and sincerely.

With thanksgiving: He wants you to give thanks to Him in advance.

Let your requests be known to God: Let him know what you need.

And the peace of God: He is a God of peace.

Which surpasses all understanding: He will give you peace that is beyond your human comprehension.

Will guard your hearts and minds through Christ Jesus: The peace that God gives you through His son Jesus Christ will guard (protect from harm and oversee) both your heart and your mind...and this is why there is no need to be anxious.

So as you're having those feelings of anxiety or concerning thoughts, you can take this scripture, think about each line, ponder what it means to you and your situation, and respond accordingly. That is one example, but you can do this with any of the scriptures that apply to your situation.

There's another key benefit to meditating on the Word of God -- it's a powerful offensive weapon! In Ephesians 6:10-18, Paul speaks about putting on the full armor of God in order to take a stand against the enemy's schemes. What is interesting is that he speaks of quite a bit of defensive gear (the belt of truth, the breastplate of righteousness, the shoes of peace, the shield of faith, the helmet of salvation), but he only speaks of one offensive weapon -- the sword, which is the Word of God. While the entire armor is important, there's only one needed weapon for offensive attack!

The enemy has no authority over the Word. Because you want to be prepared for spiritual battle, it's important to not only meditate on His Word, but also to memorize scriptures that apply to certain life or business situations you face. It's your sword and you want to have it handy as soon as you need it. Thanks to smartphones and Bible apps, you can have the Word available to you within just a moment, but sometimes you need to have certain scriptures "on the ready" without even needing to look them up.

Thank God for His Word which will always produce fruit, accomplish His purposes, and prosper everywhere He sends it (Isaiah 55:11, NLT)!

Say this prayer aloud:

"Father, I thank You for revealing Yourself to me through Your Word. I thank You that every word is tried and purified (Psalm 119:11). Thank You for equipping me with a powerful tool that gives me hope, instructs me in Your ways, and helps me to be effective at carrying out Your will in my life. I will hide Your Word in my heart and trust that each word You speak will accomplish every purpose in my life that You intend."

Day 20: Cultivating Confidence In God

"So do not throw away this confident trust in the Lord. Remember the great reward it brings you! Patient endurance is what you need now, so that you will continue to do God's will. Then you will receive all that he has promised." ~Hebrews 10:35-36 (NLT)

Throughout this devotional we have covered many characteristics and promises of God, yet we have barely scratched the surface of how absolutely amazing He is! The Word of God is full of His promises and the abundant, adventurous life He intends for you to experience with Him.

The key to experiencing life the way God intends for you to is to cultivate confidence in Him, His character, and His promises. Confidence is where power lies. Confidence reveals Heaven on earth. Whenever your expectations are low or non-existent, you're choosing a life that is void of His power and far beneath His desire for you.

Why is it that you can be confident in God? Here are a few reasons:

He cannot lie and He doesn't change His mind. What He says, He will do. What He promises, He will fulfill (Numbers 23:19).

He doesn't change. He's the same yesterday, today, and forever (Hebrews 13:8).

He is completely trustworthy. This is why the Bible urges us to trust the Lord with all our hearts instead of leaning on our own understanding. The Word says if you acknowledge Him in all your ways, He will direct your path (Proverbs 3:5).

The last thing you want to have is an unbelieving heart. If you look back to the stories of the Bible, you will see that skepticism and unbelief yield unpleasant results. The people of Nazareth missed out on miracles that Jesus desired to perform because they were plagued with unbelief (Mark 6:4-6). A generation of Israelites were shut off from the Promised Land and wandered in the wilderness for forty years because of unbelief (Hebrews 3:15-19). James referred to a doubtful and unbelieving person as unstable:

> *If you need wisdom, ask our generous God, and he will give it to you. He will not rebuke you for asking. But when you ask him, be sure that your faith is in God alone. Do not waver, for a person with divided loyalty is as unsettled as a wave of the sea that is blown and tossed by the wind. Such people should not expect anything from the Lord. Their loyalty is divided between God and the world, and they are unstable in everything they do.* (James 1:6, New Living Translation)

So how do you cultivate confidence in God? Simply expect God to be what He says He is in specific situations that you face and allow your attitude and response to Him to adjust accordingly. As a Kingdom Driven Entrepreneur, it's important to apply this practice to your business as well. For example, before walking into an important meeting or conference call you can choose to expect God to give you wisdom (as He has promised!) and thank Him ahead of time for it. You may also choose to expect God to be in control (which the Bible says He is!) and thank Him ahead of time for having your ultimate best in mind as it pertains to the result of that meeting.

Believing God isn't always easy, and part of cultivating confidence is recognizing that God knows what's best for you and ensures that all things work together for your good (Romans 8:28). In times of disappointment and even in times of pain, it's important to recognize His goodness and lean on Him even more. God will indeed provide the strength you need to endure difficult times in your life and business. None of your pain will ever be wasted.

Cultivate the habit of reminding yourself of His character as often as possible throughout your day. He is trustworthy. He cannot lie. He is always with you. He is always FOR you. He desires the best for you.

Say this prayer aloud:

"Father I thank You for delighting in me and always desiring the best for me. Help my unbelief and remove any doubts or low expectations I have of You. Help me to operate each day expecting Your best for me in every situation that I face, fully recognizing that You are sovereign and in control and that Your best may not always come in the way or timing that I think it will come."

Day 21: Enjoying the Presence of God

"I can never escape from your Spirit! I can never get away from your presence!" ~Psalm 139:7 (NLT)

Life as a Kingdom Driven Entrepreneur is quite an adventure, and the best way to live it is in daily companionship with your Heavenly Father. It's a trust walk that will certainly cost you something, but the rewards are great! Regardless of where you are in terms of your spiritual growth, there is so much more of Him to experience.

A wonderful way to walk with Him daily is to consider that the Lord is with you at all times and acknowledge His presence as often as possible in every aspect of your personal and business life. When you do this, God will use you in the most amazing and spontaneous ways that will reveal His love and power to those around you. Here are some ways you can do this in your daily life:

- Have conversations with God throughout the day. Just talk to Him like you're talking to a friend. Tell Him what's going on and then listen to what He has to share with you. Those conversations are, in fact, prayers.

- Worship Him right in the middle of your work day. Praise Him for who He is in your life and for what He is doing through you and for you. Pray or even sing in the Holy Spirit. Tell Him how good

He is. Not only does He love to hear it, but you will encourage yourself.

-   Ask God what He wants! When you're faced with a decision, simply ask Him what to do, what to say, or how to think about a situation. This is something you may already do with large decisions, but try it in smaller matters too. Remember there is no issue too small or too large -- He is concerned with it all.

-   Spend quiet time in the mornings or evenings just soaking in the presence of God, listening to some of your favorite worship music, and simply spending time with Him. Open your heart and allow Him to minister to your spirit.

-   Write your thoughts out in a journal. You can have a conversation with Him through writing!

-   When you know you'll be meeting with someone, ask God what He wants to have accomplished in the meeting. Ask Him how He wants to use you to have a positive impact on the person you're meeting with.

While it is likely that you won't consider God's presence in every single moment of your life, the more you acknowledge Him and respond accordingly, the more God encounters you will experience in your life and business. Consider Romans 12:1 (The Message):

So here's what I want you to do, God helping you: Take your everyday, ordinary life—your sleeping, eating, going-to-work, and walking-around life— and place it before God as an offering. Embracing what God does for you is the best thing you can do for him. Don't become so well-adjusted to your culture that you fit into it without even thinking.

Instead, fix your attention on God. You'll be changed from the inside out. Readily recognize what he wants from you, and quickly respond to it. Unlike the culture around you, always dragging you down to its level of immaturity, God brings the best out of you, develops well-formed maturity in you.

Enjoy the presence of your King and be open to new ways of interacting with Him daily. He loves you without measure and is the perfect companion in your Kingdom Driven entrepreneurial journey.

Say this prayer aloud:

"Father, thank You for Your grace which allows me to stay close to You. Thank You for purging me of the things that are unlike You and changing me from the inside out. You. Give me insight into the areas where I have shut You out. I welcome and need Your presence in my family. There is absolutely nothing in my life that is off limits to I welcome and need Your presence in my business. Lord, I ask for more of You in every area of my life."

About The Author

Shae Bynes is Co-Founder of Kingdom Driven Entrepreneur ™ with a mission to equip entrepreneurs of faith to build thriving businesses so they can serve their families, truly impact lives, and advance the Kingdom of God in the marketplace.

Shae has been an internet entrepreneur for over a decade and business coach to part-time entrepreneurs and real estate investors since leaving her corporate career behind in 2010. It is those experiences that prepared her for what she considers her most important work to date – equipping entrepreneurs of faith through the Kingdom Driven Entrepreneur community.

Shae is an inspiring speaker, a passionate storyteller, and an engaging teacher. Her life and business were completely transformed through the power of encountering God. She has authored or co-authored several books on the topic of God-centered business, and she has no plans of stopping any time soon.

Shae holds a Bachelor of Science degree in Computer Science from the University of South Florida and a Masters of Business Administration in Management from the University of Florida. A native Floridian, she is addicted to sunshine and happily calls the Fort Lauderdale area her home. She's a loving wife to her high school sweetheart Phil and mother of two Kingdom Driven Entrepreneurs in the making, Anisa and Nia.

Bonus Online Resources

Weekly e-zine, Kingdom Impact:
KingdomDrivenEntrepreneur.com

The Kingdom Driven Entrepreneur Podcast
KingdomDrivenEntrepreneur.com
Subscribe via iTunes or Stitcher Radio today!

Other Books for Kingdom Driven Entrepreneurs

The Kingdom Driven Entrepreneur: Doing Business God's Way (ISBN: 978-0615736129)

The Kingdom Driven Entrepreneur's Guide To Goal Setting (ISBN: 978-0615771892)

The Kingdom Driven Entrepreneur's Guide To Fearless Business Finance (ISBN: 978-0989632201)

The Kingdom Driven Entrepreneur's Guide To Holistic Health (ISBN: 978-0989632218)

The Kingdom Driven Entrepreneur's Guide To Extraordinary Leadership (Coming November 2013)

Featured Kingdom Driven Entrepreneurs in Encountering God

Below are the Kingdom Driven businesses owned by the entrepreneurs whose stories were featured in this devotional.

Bess Blanco, The Intentional Lifestyle
Faith-based Health Coaching
TheIntentionalLifestyle.com

David Burrus, David A Burrus Global
DavidABurrus.com

Jeanette Burton
Web and Graphic Designer
Jeanette.BurtonSigns.com.au

Jeff and Dawn Clark, Kingdom Called
Writing and editing services for Kingdom Builders
KingdomCalled.com

Candace Ford, CNF Ministries
Equipping Radical Leaders for the Kingdom
CNFMinistries.com

Alicia Hommon, Cake Whimzy
Cake designer and baker
CakeWhimzy.com

Maria McDavis, Genius Awesome Sauce
Digital Strategist
MariaRMcDavis.com

Lisa Miller-Baldwin, The Wonderfully Made Foundation
Empowering women and children impacted by domestic violence and homelessness
TheWonderfullyMadeFoundation.com

Alex Navas, Christian Business Academy
Business Coaching and Training
ChristianBusinessAcademy.com

Steven Washington, Secret Wealth Academy
Real Estate Education and Training
SecretWealthAcademy.com

31219776R00066

Made in the USA
Charleston, SC
09 July 2014